On The Hunt With AFRICAN LIONS

BY KRISTEN POPE

Published by The Child's World®
1980 Lookout Drive • Mankato, MN 56003-1705
800-599-READ • www.childsworld.com

Acknowledgments
The Child's World®: Mary Berendes, Publishing Director
Red Line Editorial: Design, editorial direction, and production
Photographs ©: Nejron Photo/Shutterstock Images, cover, 1; Maggy
Meyer/Shutterstock Images, 4; Red Line Editorial, 6; iStockphoto, 7, 16, 21;
Shutterstock Images, 8, 11, 15; Guido Bissattini/Shutterstock Images, 10;
Howard Klaaste/Shutterstock Images, 12; Graeme Shannon/Shutterstock
Images, 14; Colin Edwards Wildside/Shutterstock Images, 18

ISBN 9781634074476

LCCN 2015946216

Printed in the United States of America
Mankato, MN
December, 2015
PA02279

TABLE OF
CONTENTS

Chapter 1

ON THE HUNT

The sun has set over the African plains. The darkness provides good cover. Clouds cover the moon. It is the best kind of night for hunting. Five female lions sit in the darkness. They eye a herd of zebras. One small zebra wanders away from its group. The lions keep their eyes on it. Slowly the zebra walks far away from its herd. Now it is alone. It is time for the lions to act. The lions quietly get into position. They hide and wait as the zebra walks closer. They will sneak up and attack it.

The five female lions work together. They spread out. Two lions sneak around the zebra. One goes to the right. One goes to the left. Another one stays put but creeps closer. Now the zebra is surrounded.

Zebras can run very fast. But when they are circled by lions, they are in trouble. It is hard for any **prey** to escape a **pride** of lion **predators**. One lion creeps closer. She is going in for the kill. The zebra is looking the other way. Using her powerful legs, the lion

◄ **Female lions watch prey as the sun sets in Africa.**

African lions live here

▲ African lions live only in Africa.

bounds at 50 miles (80 km) per hour and jumps on the zebra. All 300 pounds (136 kg) of her lands on the zebra's back. The zebra's legs buckle. The lion clings to its prey with her long, **retractable** claws. Her jaws clamp down on its neck. The zebra squeals and kicks, desperately trying to get away. The other lions race in. One slams its paw down on the zebra's neck. The zebra can't breathe. It is bleeding. The lions wait until the zebra stops kicking.

The lions aren't far from the rest of their pride. The females drag the kill a short way. They set it next to a bush. The pride moves in to share the kill. The two male lions dig in first. Even though the females do most of the hunting, the males eat first. Males rule the pride. They rip off hunks of zebra meat and gulp it down. Blood stains their shaggy manes. Their rough tongues help rip the flesh off the bones.

Then the females get to eat. After they have their turns, there is only a little meat left. A few scraps cling to the ribs and bones. Four lion cubs slowly walk up. Now it is their turn. They get the leftovers. Not every cub gets enough to eat. Sometimes cubs starve to death. Lions are **carnivores** and only eat meat. A single zebra provides a lot of food. The pride will not need to kill another animal for three to five days.

▲ **Lions use their retractable claws to attack and cling into their prey.**

Chapter 2

DAILY LION LIFE

The sun begins to rise. It is time to find a spot to nap. The females and their cubs lie down under a tree. As the sun comes up, they doze off. Lions sleep out in the open. They do not need protection because they are top predators. Lions can spend up to 20 hours resting and sleeping each day. As the females and their cubs lie together, two males wander around the edge of the pride. A pride can have up to 40 lions in it. Most have around 13 lions. There are usually just a few males and many females.

The females and cubs lie together snoozing. One female wakes up and licks the lion to her left. The two lions rub their heads together. Another lion purrs. They all go back to sleep. A little while later, another lion stirs. The sun is hot on her. She gets up and finds a shadier spot. She settles down for another nap.

One small cub approaches his mother. The cub wants to play. He scratches at his mother with his paw. His mother doesn't stir. She ignores the cub. So he goes to the next lion and scratches

◀ **Lions can sleep out in the open because they do not need to worry about predators.**

9

▲ Lions can go four or five days without water.

her. She gives the cub a playful nudge and a lick. She is not the cub's mother, but she acts like it sometimes. The females in a pride work together to raise all of the cubs.

The sun rises higher in the sky. Hours pass. The temperature rises. It is almost noon, but the lions are still asleep. Resting is how they spend the hottest part of the day. This helps them save their energy. After last night's meal, they won't need to eat for a while. They don't even need to get up to find water. They get most of the water they need from the animals they eat.

◀ Lions are very social animals.

Chapter 3

CLAIMING THEIR TERRITORY

The playful cub climbs up on a rock. He climbs higher and looks around. In the distance, he sees some trees. Tall grass is all around. He sees one of the adult male lions walking through the tall grass. Every once in a while, the cub sees a flicker of the male's mane. The thick, reddish-brown mane surrounds the male's head. Some males have blond manes. Others have black ones. Female lions prefer males with darker manes.

The male's long body peeks out from the grass. This lion is 6 feet (1.8 m) long, but some males can be even longer. His coat is a yellow-brown color. He is hard to see in the waving grass. The color of his coat helps him blend in. It is a form of **camouflage**. The lion uses this camouflage to sneak up on its prey. His long tail curls up. It is half as long as his body. Someday, the cub will be

◀ **Only male lions grow manes.**

▲ **A lion's coat helps it blend in with tall, yellow grass.**

that big. Adult male lions can weigh 265 to 420 pounds (120 to 190 kg). Females are usually smaller than males.

The adult male walks around his pride's **territory**. It is his job to defend it. The male walks up to a rock. He urinates on it. This marks his territory. Other animals will smell it when they get close. This is a way of showing the other animals this area is claimed. A pride's territory can be 100 square miles (260 sq km).

The male jumps on top of the rock. Opening his wide mouth, he lets out a huge roar. The roar is very loud. It startles the cub. This is another way of letting animals know the area belongs to his pride. If an animal gets too close, the lion will chase it away.

The cub sees another male lion far away in the distance. That is what the pride's lion was roaring at. Male lions can be very dangerous for cubs. Sometimes they kill them. Every few years, new males take over each pride. When they arrive, the other males have to leave. But they don't want to go. Sometimes they fight to the death. If males are kicked out, they set off to find a new pride. The new males also kill any cubs with the pride. The new lion turns around. It heads away. For now.

▲ **Animals 5 miles (8 km) away can hear a lion's roar.**

Chapter 4

GROWING CUBS

Back at the pride, one female lion stirs. She is about to give birth. Every 18 to 26 months, adult females usually have a litter of cubs. The other females gather around. The female gives birth to three cubs. Most females give birth to three or four cubs at a time. Sometimes, they can have only one or two. Other times, they can have up to six.

This mother is lucky. All three of her cubs are alive. She licks each one. Each tiny newborn cub weighs about 3 pounds (1.4 kg). She keeps them close. The pride watches them closely. The young ones are very **vulnerable**. Leopards, hyenas, and other predators sometimes eat them. Fewer than half of all cubs survive their first year. Females can live for 15 to 18 years in the wild. Males usually live for 12 to 16 years.

One of the tiny newborns yawns. She has spots. As she grows, her spots will disappear. She has a lot to learn about being a lion. But her pride will teach her. They will teach her how to hunt and

◄ **Female cubs stay with their mother's pride their whole lives.**

how to get along with other lions. She will stay with her mother's pride. Male cubs only stay for about two and a half years. But the newborns are not the only cubs with the pride. Four other cubs are settled on the grass with the pride. Two of them are old enough to help with the hunt. Once the cubs are one year old, they help hunt. Lions usually hunt together. But if one is alone and has the chance, it will hunt alone.

One of the older cubs wanders off. He perches on a rock. He is only a year and a half old. A bird is resting on a low tree branch. He sneaks up on it. Crouching down, he pounces into action. He leaps through the air. With a flash of feathers, the bird takes off. While females do most of the pride's hunting, males must still learn to hunt. They need these skills when they set off to find a new pride.

One of the cubs with the pride stretches out in the shade. He is almost as big as an adult now. He is just over two years old. Soon he will head off on his own. He will look for his own pride. Since lions have such large territories, it will not be easy. He will have to travel far to find one. While he is looking for a pride, he will have to kill his own food. Or he can steal what hyenas and wild dogs kill.

◀ **Lion cubs are born with spots.**

Once he finds a pride, he will have to drive away the males in that pride. It is not an easy task. Many times, males will join with their brothers or cousins to look for a pride to take over together. He might wait a little longer so his younger brother can go with him.

Off in the distance, a giraffe eats leaves in a tree. When the lion cub is larger, he will be able to hunt giraffes. He will also hunt wildebeests, impalas, wild hogs, and even buffalos. But for now, he must learn to hunt smaller prey.

A lion cub crouches down low before pouncing, ▶ or leaping, at its prey.

GLOSSARY

camouflage (KAM-uh-flahzh): Camouflage is a disguise or natural coloring an animal has that makes it look like its surroundings in order to hide. The lion's fur is a good camouflage so its prey can't see it coming.

carnivores (KAHR-nuh-vors): Carnivores are animals that eat meat. Lions are carnivores.

predators (PRED-uh-terz): Predators are animals that eat other animals. Lions are top predators.

prey (PRAY): Prey are animals that are eaten by other animals. Zebras are good prey for lions.

pride (pride): A pride is a group of lions that work and live together. Male lions rule the pride.

retractable (re-TRACT-uh-buhl): Something that is retractable can be drawn in and out. The lion's claws are retractable.

territory (TER-i-tor-ee): A territory is an area of land a group controls. Lions mark and protect their territory.

vulnerable (VUHL-nur-uh-buhl): To be vulnerable means to be in a position where something could be easily damaged. Young lions are vulnerable to leopards, hyenas, and other predators.

TO LEARN MORE

Books

Blake, Carly. *Big Cats*. New York: Windmill Books, 2015.

Glaser, Rebecca. *Lions Roar*. Mankato, MN: Amicus Ink, 2016.

Owen, Ruth. *Lions*. New York: Windmill Books, 2012.

Web Sites

Visit our Web site for links about African lions:
childsworld.com/links

Note to Parents, Teachers, and Librarians: We routinely verify our Web links to make sure they are safe and active sites. So encourage your readers to check them out!

SELECTED BIBLIOGRAPHY

"African Lion." *Woodland Park Zoo*. Woodland Park Zoo, 2015. Web. 15 June 2015.

"Basic Facts about Lions." *Defenders of Wildlife*. Defenders of Wildlife, 2015. Web. 4 June 2015.

"Lion Facts." *Smithsonian National Zoological Park*. Smithsonian Institution, n.d. Web. 6 June 2015.

INDEX

ABOUT THE AUTHOR

Kristen Pope is a writer and editor with years of experience working in national and state parks and museums. She has a master's degree in natural resources and has taught people of all ages about science and the environment. She has even coaxed reluctant insect-lovers to pet Madagascar hissing cockroaches.